100

THINGS TO DO IN

AUSTIN

BEFORE YOU

DIE

D0733857

100
THINGS TO DO IN
AUSTIN
BEFORE YOU
DIE

• •

KRISTY OWEN

REEDY PRESS
St. Louis, Missouri

To Austinites everywhere and one special sister, Ali Owen; without her this journey would have never started.

I'd also like to give a special thank you to my mom and dad who have been endlessly supportive and have always encouraged me to pursue my dreams. I love you and couldn't ask for more.

Copyright © 2014 by Reedy Press, LLC

Reedy Press
PO Box 5131
St. Louis, MO 63139, USA
www.reedypress.com

Library of Congress Control Number: 201493811

ISBN: 978-1-935806-71-4

Design by Jill Halpin

Printed in the United States of America
16 17 18   5 4 3

Please note that websites, phone numbers, addresses, and company names are subject to change or cancellation. We did our best to relay the most accurate information available, but due to circumstances beyond our control, please do not hold us liable for misinformation. When exploring new destinations, please do your homework before you go.

For more information, upcoming author events, and book signings, please visit us on Facebook at www.365ThingsAustin.com.

CONTENTS

PREFACE

Many years ago, I found myself sitting in my freshman dorm room as my parents returned to Houston. Preparing to embark on the journey of a lifetime, I was alone in a city that I'd only visited once or twice before. Over the next four years I found myself on endless adventures, and even after my time at the University of Texas concluded, I knew I wouldn't be leaving this amazing city anytime soon.

I've always been big on New Year's resolutions. So, as I looked towards a new decade in late 2009, a goal of mine was to get out and try new things in Austin. I found myself constantly going back to the same places, bars, and restaurants, time and time again, and while they were excellent I felt it would be advantageous to try new places and expand my knowledge of the city I'd grown to love. My blog—365 Things To Do in Austin, Texas—was born on New Year's Day, 2010, and it was the beginning of a wild ride that I never saw coming.

If there's one thing I've learned, it's that Austin is always changing. Busy fighting to hold onto the weirdness that draws so many people here, while dealing with the growing pains that come with an extremely rapid increase in population.

After blogging on over a thousand "things to do in Austin," this is a list of a hundred tried-and-true activities that I think both locals and visitors will benefit from experiencing. Enjoy the ride.

FOOD &
DRINK

Behold, here is the menu itself.
Shhh! It's a secret!

• •

JACK OF CLUBS – a fried egg, potatoes, black beans, crispy corn tortilla strips, shredded cheese, cilantro, sour cream, and Diablo. Served on a flour tortilla.

ACE OF SPADES – a jalapeno sausage link, grilled brisket, a fried egg, green chile queso, cilantro, cotija cheese, sour cream, and Diablo. Served on a flour tortilla.

TRAILER PARK HILLBILLY STYLE – fried chicken, chorizo, chopped bacon, green chilies, green chile queso, shredded cheese, pico de gallo, pablano ranch on the side. Served on a flour tortilla.

MAD COW – fajita beef, black beans, grilled corn, jack cheese, creamy chipotle, and cilantro. Served on a flour tortilla.

THE HIPSTER – panko fried tuna with green chilies, chopped bacon, black bean relish, cotija cheese, avocado sauce, cilantro, and a wedge of lime. Served on a flour tortilla.

THE MATADOR – chopped brisket, grilled jalapeno, pickled onions, jack cheese, avocado, sour cream, and cilantro. Served with tomatillo sauce on a crisp corn tortilla wrapped in a flour tortilla.

GREEN CHILE PORK MISSIONARY STYLE – green chile pork, pickled onions, guacamole, jack cheese, cilantro, creamy chipotle on a crisp corn tortilla inside a flour tortilla.

• •

Make sure to complete your order with Torchy's queso.
No trip to Torchy's is complete without it.

ORDER OFF THE SECRET
MENU AT TORCHY'S TACOS

You've probably heard about Torchy's Tacos and their legendary "damn good" tacos, but did you know that they have a secret menu? Thanks to the Internet, you can find just about anything, including the top-secret menu. The first time you order from this secret menu you might be a bit anxious. After proudly declaring that I wanted an "Ace of Spades" for the first time, I was worried that I would get a confused look or possibly even laughed at, but nope, it was as smooth as any other order I had placed. Upon completion, you'll feel as though you've joined some underground society of true Torchy's Tacos fans.

various locations
torchystacos.com

BAR HOP
ON RAINEY STREET

The Rainey Street district proves the saying "what is old is new again." Not long ago, this was a row of older homes that sat on the outskirts of downtown. Thanks to the Rainey Street Queen, Bridget Dunlap, who had the vision to transform this old neighborhood into an alternative to the existing bar districts downtown, it's become one of the city's best spots to grab a drink. The bars still feature many of the bungalow-style characteristics and charm of the original homes, and the backyards-turned-patios are some of the best outdoor drinking spots in the city. Dunlap's latest contribution to Rainey opened during SXSW 2014—an elaborate bar made of recycled shipping containers.

raineystbars.com

VISIT THE
WHOLE FOODS FLAGSHIP STORE

The Whole Foods on South Lamar is a culinary amusement park. What other grocery store in America would you be comfortable bringing a date to? Offerings include the ultimate salad bar, a sushi bar, a pizzeria, a gelato shop, and even a beer and wine bar dubbed Bar Lamar.

524 N. Lamar Blvd.
(512) 542-2200
wholefoodsmarket.com

TASTE *TOP CHEF*
WINNER PAUL QUI'S CREATIONS

Long before *Top Chef* fame, Paul Qui was busy making a name for himself in Austin's culinary circuit. He first started turning heads at Uchiko, and then went on to open East Side King at Liberty Bar on East Sixth. Side note: This place is still one of the best trailers in town; try the poor qui buns and beet fries. After several more trailers and cable TV fame, he finally opened the much-anticipated Qui. That's where you'll usually find him these days if you want to catch him on the job. Qui is amazing, but comes with a pretty hefty price tag. I recommend the cote de boeuf. It's a $150 steak that is meant to be shared between two to six people, and it's worth every penny. If you don't want to spend the big bucks, then pay homage to where it all started at one of his East Side King locations. You most likely won't have a celebrity chef sighting, but you can experience the craft that made Paul Qui famous.

Qui
1600 E. 6th St., (512) 436-9626
quiaustin.com

East Side King at Liberty Bar
1618 E. 6th St.
eskaustin.com

There's also an ESK at Hole in the Wall, ESK South Lamar

Thai-Kun at Whisler's
1816 E. 6th St.

Franklin BBQ Tip:

The line starts early at this spot and gets long quickly. I've had my best luck getting there around 11:00 A.M. on a Tuesday or Wednesday.

SEARCH FOR
THE CITY'S BEST BBQ

The BBQ scene in Austin has experienced a renaissance in the last few years. Making the drive out to Lockhart for their offerings is still worth the trip, but we have a handful of places right here in town that you should check off your list first.

Franklin BBQ
900 E. 11th St., (512) 653-1187, franklinbarbecue.com

John Mueller Meat Co.
2500 E. 6th St., johnmuellermeatco.com/home

la Barbecue
1906 E. Cesar Chavez, (512) 605-9696, labarbecue.com

The Blue Ox BBQ (Buzz Mill Coffee's Courtyard)
1505 Town Creek Dr., (512) 537-2047, blueoxbarbecue.com

Micklethwait Craft Meats
1309 Rosewood Ave., (512) 791-5961, craftmeats.com

Kerlin BBQ
1700 E. Cesar Chavez, (512) 412-5588, kerlinbbq.com

TRACK DOWN
THE VERY BEST BREAKFAST TACOS

Attempting to declare one breakfast taco spot "best in the city" will incite an argument with a level of intensity usually reserved for talks on politics or religion. Several spots that routinely come up in the forums I can vouch for firsthand:

Veracruz All Natural
1704 E. Cesar Chavez
(512) 412-5588

East Seventh Eats
1403 E. 7th St.

Radio Coffee & Beer
4208 Manchaca Rd.

El Primo Taco Trailer
2101 S. 1st St.
(512) 227-5060

Joe's Bakery and Coffee Shop
2305 E. 7th St.
(512) 472-0017
joesbakery.com

Amaya's Taco Village
5804 Interstate 35
(512) 458-2531
amayastacovillage.com

Taco Deli
various locations
tacodeli.com

USE THE CODE WORD
FOR ENTRY AT MIDNIGHT COWBOY

This is one of Austin's best kept secrets. From the mind behind Alamo Drafthouse comes this gem hidden in the middle of "dirty" Sixth Street. Reservations are required, and you'll be given secret instructions on how to gain entry. Identified only by a red porch light out front, finding the venue is part of the adventure! Once inside, you'll feel like you're in a speakeasy from the 1920s. The drinks are exceptional, the bartenders are beyond knowledgeable, and the drink menu is expansive. Try at least one of the table-side prepared cocktails, and keep in mind that there is a two-drink minimum per person.

313 E. 6th St.
(512) 843-2715
midnightcowboymodeling.com

STUFF YOURSELF
ON AN AUSTIN EATS FOOD TOUR

Both locals and visitors enjoy this behind-the-scenes look at some of Austin's best restaurants. One of my favorite tours is the Eastside option. It takes you to several awesome food trailers, some great brick-and-mortar restaurants, and a brewery! They offer walking, van, and even electronic bike tours. I highly recommend the electronic bike option, unless it's triple-digit heat, then the AC in the van is just too good to pass up.

austineatsfoodtours.com

9

TOUR THE AMY'S
ICE CREAMS PRODUCTION FACILITY

Started in 1984 with a hot check, Amy's now dominates the ice cream game in Austin, Texas. With over three hundred flavors and dozens of locations, the homegrown ice cream chain has become a local favorite.

With the tour, you'll get a behind-the-scenes peek at everything that goes into each scoop. Tours are free but must be scheduled a month in advance. Sign up by calling 512-458-3188.

2109 Northland Dr.
(512) 458-3188
amysicecreams.com/tours

GRAB A CUP
OF JO'S COFFEE ON SOUTH CONGRESS

I'm not sure if it's the awesome coffee or the over-photographed "I love you so much" graffiti art on the side of the building that makes this a destination for locals and tourists alike. Most mornings the line wraps around the side of the building as customers anxiously await their caffeine fix.

They have a prime location, right in the heart of South Congress Avenue, and no one can resist snapping a photo in front of the famed graffiti. I myself am guilty of this as well; I've posted up for pictures with friends, family, and even my dog on separate occasions.

1300 South Congress Ave.
(512) 444-3800
joscoffee.com/congress/jossouthcongress.htm

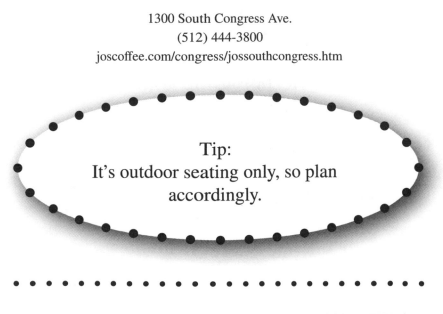

Tip:
It's outdoor seating only, so plan accordingly.

Some of Our Favorite Queso Destinations:

Matt's El Rancho
(The Bob Armstrong Dip)
2613 S. Lamar Blvd.
(512) 462-9333
mattselrancho.com

Magnolia Café
(Mag Mud)
various locations
themagnoliacafe.com

Polvo's Mexican Restaurant
2004 S. 1st St.
(512) 441-5446
polvosaustin.com

Kerbey Lane Café
(Kerbey Queso)
various locations
kerbeylanecafe.com

Torchy's Tacos
various locations
torchystacos.com

QUESO, QUESO,

Time spent in Austin isn't complete without consuming a few pounds of the gooey cheese and salsa mix that Texans call queso. This uniquely southern dish can be served in countless ways; sometimes it's just plain melted cheese, while other times it's filled with avocado, some form of beef, onions, cilantro, tomatoes, and more. Each place has its own twist on this classic appetizer.

Queso is such a treat that each summer the Mohawk on Red River hosts a "queso-off" where individuals, companies, and restaurants compete to be crowned queso champ.

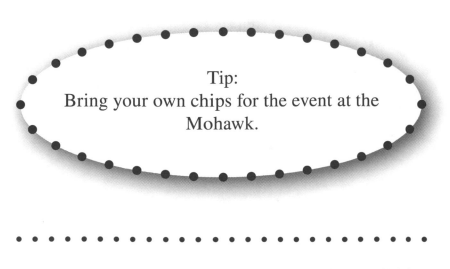

Tip:
Bring your own chips for the event at the Mohawk.

SIP
SPECIALTY COCKTAILS
AT HOTEL SAN JOSE

Sipping cocktails on the patio at this bungalow-style hotel in the heart of South Congress is sure to give you a taste of true Austin culture.

The courtyard has a private, Zen-like feel where hours seem to fly by. They have wine, beer, cocktails, and a light food menu. Try one of the house specialties; while they change seasonally, you can't really go wrong with any of their concoctions. They often have live music for you to enjoy as well.

If you're into celebrity sightings, this trendy boutique hotel is a mainstay for the stars when they come to Austin.

1316 South Congress Ave.
(512) 444-7322
sanjosehotel.com

CAPTURE THE SUNSET
AT THE OASIS

Okay, it's a bit touristy and the food is nothing to write home about, but there's no doubt that the Oasis provides one of the best sunset views in the city. The breathtaking scene is spread across multiple decks 450 feet above Lake Travis.

A little bit of history: in June 2005, lightning struck the restaurant, a fire ensued and burned 80 percent of the decks. Three days later they reopened to customers and salvaged the remaining deck space. They immediately began to rebuild and the property is now bigger and better than ever. They can now seat up to 2,500 people, making it the largest outdoor restaurant in Texas.

The sunset is so spectacular that each year they host a sunset photo contest. Professionals and novices alike try to get the winning shot.

6550 Comanche Trl.
(512) 266-2442
oasis-austin.com

TAKE
THE MAN VS. FOOD CHALLENGE
AT JUAN IN A MILLION

Get ready for a handshake from the owner when you walk through the door at Juan In A Million. The warm welcome is a trademark of this East Austin favorite.

Their claim to fame is the Don Juan—a massive taco stuffed with eggs, potatoes, bacon, and cheese. You'll notice that we didn't put this place on our top picks for tacos. The allure here is the legacy and the price; you can get a huge taco (in reality you can make three or four tacos from one Don Juan) for just a couple of bucks.

If you've ever seen *Man vs. Food* on the Travel Channel, Adam (the host) takes on eight Don Juans in an attempt to beat the current record. He didn't even come close, finishing only four. How many can you chow down?

2300 East Cesar Chavez St.
(512) 472-3872
juaninamillion.com

DO DINNER
PAST YOUR BEDTIME

Throw caution to the wind, stay up late, and go eat somewhere past 2 A.M. This may only appeal to you if you're leaving the bars or you're an insomniac, but there really is something unique about a joint that never closes. Here are your best bets for dining around the clock in the Capital City.

La Mexicana Bakery
Get a torta or breakfast tacos, with a side of the best looking pastry in the display case.
1924 South 1st Street, (512) 443-6369, la-mexicana-bakery.com

24 Diner
Do yourself a favor and try their chicken and waffles; they're an acceptable meal any day, anytime.
600 N. Lamar Blvd., (512) 472-5400, 24diner.com

Kerbey Lane
Order the Kerbey queso and a stack of one of their pancakes and you'll be all set.
various locations, kerbeylanecafe.com

Magnolia Café
various locations, themagnoliacafe.com

TRY LOCAL
CRAFTS ON A BREWERY TOUR

Austin is on the cutting edge of the microbrewery revolution. All of the local breweries want to showcase their prized potions, so they offer tours that are open to the public. There's certainly a science to the brewing process and no two companies' processes are alike, so every brewery's tour is different. Breweries are located all over Austin and throughout the Texas Hill Country. Most tours occur on weekends and range in price from free to $10. Here are a few breweries to check off your list.

(512) Brewing Company
407 Radam Ln., (512) 707-2337, 512brewing.com

Hops & Grain
507 Calles St., (512) 914-2467, hopsandgrain.com

Jester King Brewery
13187 Fitzhugh Rd., (512) 537-5100, jesterkingbrewery.com

Live Oak Brewing Company
3301 E. 5th St., (512) 385-2299, liveoakbrewing.com

Thirsty Planet Brewing
11160 Circle Dr., (512) 579-0679, thirstyplanet.net

GIVE IN TO
YOUR SWEET TOOTH AT
BIG TOP CANDY SHOP

Welcome to the Disneyland of candy shops. This place makes me feel like I found the golden ticket!

They have everything you would expect from an old-time candy shop. You feel like you're lost in a wonderland of chocolate, Pixy Stix, gumballs, jelly beans, and countless things that I never even knew existed—chocolate covered bacon anyone? Be sure to save room for one of their handmade milkshakes.

Walk in and you'll truly understand the expression "feeling like a kid in a candy store."

1706 South Congress Ave.
(512) 462-2220
bigtopcandyshop.tumblr.com

CUT THE CHEESE
AT ANTONELLI'S

It doesn't matter if you're a true cheese aficionado or a more casual cheese enthusiast; an evening at one of Antonelli's cheese classes is a must. The classes take place across the street from Antonelli's storefront (also worth checking out) in the Cheese House, a historic Austin building that just celebrated its one hundredth anniversary.

Be prepared for an evening of all things cheese. You'll hear cheese stories, learn some history, and of course enjoy tons of samples. You'll leave with an awareness of new cheeses and plenty of cheese anecdotes. Be ready to showcase your new-found knowledge the next time you're entertaining.

500 Park Blvd.
(512) 531-9610
antonellischeese.com/cheese-classes

Tip:

You can opt for the wine/beer pairings
with the class, but I'd recommend
bringing your own booze
as that is also an option.

Tip:

It doesn't have to be Valentine's Day to order the heart-shaped pizza; it makes a great gift anytime. Also, if you're hosting a party to watch the game they make football-shaped pizzas as well!

FALL IN LOVE
WITH MANGIA PIZZA'S
HEART-SHAPED PIZZA

Mangia Pizza's heart-shaped pizza is a favorite tradition for even the anti-romantics out there. Founded in 1988, it's been an Austin favorite ever since. Think Chicago-style pizza goodness in a heart shape. They also have traditional and thin crust pizzas, but the Chicago-style is what they're known for.

Really, what says romance more than a heart-shaped pizza and a cold beer?

8012 Mesa Dr.
(512) 349-2126
mangiapizza.com

BURGERS, BURGERS, BURGERS

There's no way to declare a "best burger in Austin," so it's best to try an array of famous Austin places. These are some of my favorites that are consistently mentioned in top ten lists:

Hopdoddy
1400 S. Congress Ave., (512) 243-7505
2438 W. Anderson Ln., (512) 467-2337
hopdoddy.com

*Beware: The long lines will make you feel like you're waiting in line at Disneyland, but it's well worth it.

Tip:
The bar offers full service,
so if you can score seats at
the bar, you can skip the line.

Hut's Hamburgers
807 W. 6th St.
(512) 472-0693
hutsfrankandangies.com

Dirty Martin's
2808 Guadalupe St.
(512) 477-3173
dirtymartins.com

Counter Café
626 N. Lamar Blvd.
(512) 708-8800
countercafe.com

Casino El Camino
517 E. 6th St.
(512) 469-9330
casinoelcamino.net

P. Terry's
various locations
pterrys.com

AUSTIN CHRONICLE
HOT SAUCE FESTIVAL

The only thing hotter than the Austin weather in late August is the annual Hot Sauce Festival. In Texas, good salsa is equally as important to residents as good BBQ.

This contest has been running for over twenty years and has become the world's largest hot sauce festival. Local restaurants, individuals, and commercial bottlers all enter this competition in hopes of being named first in their category. Bring your appetite and possibly sweatbands.

Admission to the festival is always free with a donation to the local food bank.

austinchronicle.com/gyrobase/Market/HotSauce/

SETTLE
THE SNO-BEACH VS. CASEY'S
NEW ORLEANS SNOWBALLS DEBATE

With an annual average of over 300 days of sunshine, staying cool is very important in Austin. Snow cones are one of my favorite ways to cool off, and there are two hot spots in town that will really satisfy your shaved ice craving.

Casey's New Orleans Snowballs
808 East 51st St.
caseys-snowballs.com

Sno-Beach
3402 Guadalupe St.
snobeachatx.com

Tip:
Both establishments are
cash only.

PROWL THE STREETS
FOR PRIZED PIZZA

The fourth food offering that Austin does really well besides BBQ, tacos, and burgers is pizza. The same rule applies: there's no holy grail. Take this as bittersweet news . . . it means that you have to sample several of the best before picking your favorite.

Home Slice Pizza
1415 South Congress Ave.
homeslicepizza.com

East Side Pies
1401 Rosewood Ave.
(512) 524-0933
eastsidepies.com

Salvation Pizza
624 W. 34th St.
(512) 535-0076
salvationpizza.com

Via 313
111 E. 6th St.
(512) 535-0076
via313.com

Backspace
507 San Jacinto Blvd.
(512) 474-9899
thebackspace-austin.com

"Random fact: In 1934, future president Lyndon Johnson met his future wife at the Driskill dining room for their first date."

EXPERIENCE
THE DRISKILL GRILL

This unique Austin landmark needs to be experienced by everyone at least once. The food is exquisite, the service is the best in town, and the setting is one of a kind. All that being said, it's not cheap, so know that going in.

The Driskill Hotel is full of history. It has a certain charm about it, and there are more than a few stories about the place being haunted.

604 Brazos St.
(512) 391-7162
driskillgrill.com

TEST THE TRAILER
EATERY SCENE

The trailer eatery scene is huge in Austin, and there's a never-ending stream of new trailers popping up everyday. Your mind will be blown at all the different options you can get right from a trailer. Here are some must eats:

Hey! . . . You Gonna Eat or What?

Get the Monte Cristo. It is life changing.
1720 Barton Springs Rd., (512) 296-3547
heyyougonnaeatorwhat.com

Way South Philly

1209 E. 6th St., (512) 771-6969
waysouthphilly.wordpress.com

Via 313 Pizza

1111 E. 6th St., (512) 939-1927, via313.com

Blue Ox BBQ

1501 Town Creek Dr., (512) 537-2047
bbqfoodtruckaustin.com

la Barbecue

1906 E. Cesar Chavez, (512) 605-9696
labarbecue.com

Gourdough's

1503 S. 1st St.
(512) 707-1050, gourdoughs.com

The Peached Tortilla

(Location is always changing;
follow them on social media for a schedule.)
thepeachedtortilla.com

Burro Cheese Kitchen

1221 South Congress Ave., (512) 865-7730
burrocheesekitchen.com

HAVE SOME COLD ONES
AT CRAFT PRIDE

This mecca of Texas craft beer sits at the far end of Rainey Street. They have dozens of beers on tap from around Austin and the rest of the state. This is a must-do for any beer aficionado. Not a beer fan? Try one of their locally bottled ciders.

Also, be sure to check out the Detroit-style pizza trailer on their patio; Via 313 offers the best deep-dish pizza in the city.

61 Rainey St.
(512) 428-5571
craftprideaustin.com

MUSIC & ENTERTAINMENT

Tip:

If you want to be on the cutting edge of the next Master Pancake, keep an eye on their schedule as they do "practice runs" every few months. They're typically on the Monday before a new feature.

DINNER, DRINKS, AND
MASTER PANCAKE AT
ALAMO DRAFTHOUSE

Alamo Drafthouse was a pioneer of the "dine-in" movie theater concept in Austin, and now I can't imagine watching a movie any other way. To get the full Alamo Drafthouse experience though, you have to go to a Master Pancake showing. What is Master Pancake, you ask? It is pure theatrical awesomeness. They take a movie—*Top Gun,* for example—and have two live comedians cracking jokes and mocking the entire film (if you're a fan of Mystery Science Theater, you're familiar with the concept). You don't even have to be familiar with the movie to laugh until your stomach hurts. It's truly one of the most unique movie-going experiences you can have.

various locations
drafthouse.com/Austin

SCORE TICKETS
TO AN ACL LIVE TAPING

Austin City Limits is the longest-running music program in television history, airing weekly on PBS. *Time* magazine recently named it one of the ten most influential music programs of all time. Musical greats such as Willie Nelson, B.B. King, and Radiohead have all performed here, along with countless other artists across every genre. No seat in the theater is more than seventy-five feet from the stage. The thing is, you're going to have to rely on sheer luck to score tickets to a taping as they're dispersed through a lottery system. Luckily, the lottery is free to enter; just follow ACL Live on Facebook and/or Twitter, and about a week before a taping they'll announce the sign-up. Enter your email, pray, and wait for a response. Winners are chosen at random two to three days before the show. The cameras and the legacy of ACL Live make these intimate shows a lot of fun. If you aren't chosen, you can now stream the tapings live online. It's obviously not the same experience, but it's better than missing one of your favorite acts because you weren't lucky enough to win!

ACL Live at the Moody Theater
310 W. 2nd St., Willie Nelson Blvd.
acltv.com

CATCH A SHOW
AT ESTHER'S FOLLIES

It's hard to put into words what exactly happens nightly at Esther's Follies. I will say that it's equal parts comedy and magic show. They're able to incorporate everything from local Austin political mumbo jumbo to Hollywood celebrity mockery. The show is always up to date with the latest in news, pop culture, and wit. Windows looking out onto 6th Street set the backdrop for the stage, adding even more charm and ambiance. Actors often take to the sidewalk on the other side of the glass to bring the energy of 6th Street into the theatre. The show is constantly changing, so you'll never see the same show twice!

525 East 6th St.
(512) 320-0553
esthersfollies.com

DANCE, DRINK, OR
DO BOTH AT DONN'S DEPOT

Donn's Depot is a bar made out of an actual train depot that was part of the Missouri Pacific (MoPac) railroad line. Since opening in 1972, not much has changed with this venue. It's the type of place that bridges the generation gap; you'll find couples in their seventies sharing the dance floor with folks that are young enough to be their grandchildren. The music is a good mix of '50s and '60s country, rock 'n' roll, and classic tunes that will have you tapping your feet all night long. The eclectic décor and unique crowd somehow embody everything that makes Austin good. It's the type of place that no matter how long it's been since your last visit, it's still exactly the way you remember it. Oh, and they always have free freshly made popcorn! Ladies, be sure to check out the restroom; just trust me on this one, it has more character than you can imagine.

1600 W. 5th St.
(512) 478-0336
donnsdepot.com

GET YOUR GROOVE ON
WITH A GOSPEL BRUNCH
AT STUBB'S BBQ

Stubb's is easily one of the best music venues in town, and that's saying something in the Live Music Capital of the World! On Sundays they host their famous gospel brunch, complete with a buffet of breakfast items, a Bloody Mary bar, and a side of live music.

Check their website for artist information and to see what upcoming performances they have planned.

801 Red River St.
(512) 480-8341
stubbsaustin.com

AUSTIN CITY LIMITS – Two-weekend festival in the fall that covers all genres of music, probably the most popular of Austin's music festivals.

FUN FUN FUN FEST – This festival in late fall quite possibly takes the crown as the most "fun" of the festivals. Incorporating everything from live music, comedy, and BMX to local art. "Fun Fest," as locals refer to it, always proves to be a wild weekend.
funfunfunfest.com

SXSW – This festival happens annually in March and attracts more international acts than any other festival in the United States. This is the one to go to if you're looking to see big names and discover what's next on the music scene.
sxsw.com/music

AUSTIN REGGAE FESTIVAL (MARLEY FEST) – The name speaks for itself and the festival happens annually in the spring. Admission for the festival is typically a canned food donation that the organizers pass on to the Capital Area Food Bank.
austinreggaefest.com

AUSTIN URBAN MUSIC FESTIVAL – This spring festival celebrates jazz, soul, R&B, hip-hop, and more.
austinurbanmusicfestival.com

ATTEND
A MUSIC FESTIVAL

Austin loves its live music, so it comes as no surprise that this city is known as the Live Music Capital of the World. There's a festival for just about every genre, so check the lineups when they're announced to see which ones are right for you.

aclfestival.com

CATCH
A PELIGROSA SHOW

The Peligrosa crew puts on the longest-running Latin dance party in Austin. Peligrosa is a collective of DJs, musicians, and visual artists who are all extremely talented individually; put them together and you won't find a single person in the building standing still.

A few months ago, the mayor of Austin officially declared August 8th as "Peligrosa Day," to honor what the group has done for the live music scene in the city. Check their blog for upcoming shows, and trust me when I say that regardless of what style of music you're into, you'll certainly have a blast at a Peligrosa show!

peligrosablog.com

FREE SUMMER MUSICAL
AT ZILKER

Austin is a city alive with culture and you don't need to dress up and spend a week's paycheck to enjoy a good musical. For over fifty-five years, Zilker Theatre Productions has put on a free musical in the park. Past productions have included *Annie*, *Little Shop of Horrors*, *Footloose*, *The Sound of Music*, *West Side Story*, and other Broadway classics.

Grab a blanket, pack a picnic, and grab some beverages for an evening of first-class entertainment. The show is truly top notch; and the props, costumes, and talent are nothing short of remarkable. It's a treat each year that helps Austinites through the dog days of summer.

Zilker Hillside Theatre at Zilker Park
2301 Barton Springs Rd., zilker.org

Musicals run Thursday–Sunday
mid-June through mid-August.

TEXAS
ROLLERGIRLS BOUT

Don't mess with Texas, especially the women. This raved-about experience is worth the (small) price of admission. Intense would be an understatement; once the whistle blows and the bout is underway, these girls take no prisoners as they race around the derby track.

They pride themselves on being family friendly; if you get there early, the girls are normally around to take pictures with fans and to sign autographs.

texasrollergirls.org

Get your tickets early
as most bouts sell out!
Season runs February to August.

CONTINENTAL CLUB

This historic live music venue on South Congress is an Austin institution for music lovers from all walks of life. The small space makes for an engaging experience, as you're rarely more than a few feet away from the stage. You never know who you will run into on the dance floor or who may post up on the bar stool beside you.

If timing works out, go to one of the Elvis tribute shows. They run twice a year, once on his birthday and another on the day he died. Ted Roddy and his band pay homage to the King in a one-of-a-kind show. The set covers everything, starting from his early years and finishing with a Vegas-style stage show.

1315 South Congress Ave.
(512) 441-2444
continentalclub.com/Austin.html

GET THE ULTIMATE VIEW
FROM ABOVE ON A CIRCUIT OF THE AMERICAS TOWER TOUR

In 2012 Austin became host for the United States Grand Prix. With the race came construction of a world-class racetrack and venue. As the saying goes, "everything is bigger in Texas," and this racetrack is no exception. Even if racing isn't your cup of tea, watching anything from the 251-foot tower is pretty spectacular. The tower offers 360-degree views of the racetrack and an unparalleled view of downtown. A portion of the observation tower's floor is made of seven-inch-thick plexiglass that you can stand on, jump on, pose on for photos, or use to just watch the cars whiz around hundreds of feet below. Use one of the two 419-step staircases or a high-speed elevator that takes only thirty seconds to get to the top. Go here if you're looking to conquer a fear of heights!

Race weekend tours normally run $20, cash.

If there isn't a race or event taking place, you can schedule a tour through Circuit of the Americas; however, going to the top during a race is a real treat.

circuitoftheamericas.com/articles/tours-now-available

THE PARAMOUNT

The Paramount is great for catching a formal live production or a casual movie in an elegant setting.

Built in 1915, the theatre has hosted greats such as Houdini, Willie Nelson, Billy Joel, and the Marx Brothers. While the theatre underwent a restoration in the 1970s, the charm and character that made it such a special venue are still evident in every visit.

713 Congress Ave.
(512) 472-5470
austintheatre.org

CATCH A FLICK
IN THE PARK

In a city that sees over three hundred days of sunshine a year, you can imagine that Austinites spend their fair share of time outdoors. So movies under the stars come as no surprise. Big screen experts Alamo Drafthouse bring out their massive outdoor screen and the city puts on a movie night right in downtown Austin. Many moviegoers pack their own snacks and the free admission makes for a cheap evening of Austin amusement. You can bring Fido along as well!

Parking is dicey near Republic Square Park, so biking or taking public transportation are your best options.

Republic Square Park
422 Guadalupe St.
austinparks.org/moviesinthepark.html

TAKE A SPIN
AT PLAYLAND SKATE CENTER

Playland Skate Center is a classic, old-time skating rink. They have it all: light shows, a fog machine, and a DJ. Back in the day, that was all you needed; life couldn't get much better.

If you want to hit the rink with adults only, check them out on Tuesday evenings and let the good times roll.

8822 McCann Dr.
playlandskatecenter.net/

GO NUTS
AT THE PECAN STREET FESTIVAL

The biannual Pecan Street Festival is one of Austin's longest-running festivals.

It's like a huge carnival, and it's actually the largest art festival in Central Texas. Local musicians play throughout the day, and there are more arts and crafts stands than you can imagine. It's a huge street fair with kids activities, jewelry, giant turkey legs, and all kinds of uniquely Austin attractions.

In case you're wondering, 6th Street used to be named Pecan Street, hence the name Pecan Street Festival.

oldpecanstreetfestival.com

Admission to the festival is always free.

BLUES ON THE GREEN

This is the city's longest-running free music series.

The classic series happens every summer, and there's nothing quite like taking in the sunset while listening to some live music with downtown as the backdrop. It's pretty incredible.

Blues on the Green veterans know the drill, but for first-time attendees, here's the rundown: You can bring in two factory-sealed water bottles (you should), blankets, chairs, and your dog (must be on a leash at all times). They have plenty of food vendors set up in case you get hungry.

The series runs every other Wednesday through the summer.

Zilker Park
2100 Barton Springs Rd.

Tip:

You cannot buy alcohol on the premises,
but the venue is BYOB.

TRAVEL BACK IN TIME
AT THE BLUE STARLITE
MINI URBAN DRIVE-IN

Hello memory lane! Grab your significant other and head out for a night of old-fashioned fun under the stars. This '60s-style outdoor theatre is just east of downtown and only has about forty-five car slots per showing, hence the "mini" in their name. However, this quaint drive-in is the perfect place for some good clean fun. No car, no problem; for $5 you can bike or walk in.

The Blue Starlite shows classic movies, indie films, and everything in between. They also host double-feature theme nights that are always a blast. The concession stand serves up typical theatre grub, but you're also free to bring your own snacks.

1901 E. 51st St.
bluestarlitedrivein.com

CACTUS CAFÉ

The Cactus Café is a small bar and live music venue on the University of Texas campus. It's known for its intimate setting and great acoustics. It's also the only place on campus that you can (legally) purchase alcohol. Jason Mraz, the Dixie Chicks, and the Black Crowes have all graced the stage.

In 2010 the university announced that they would close the café, but after a ton of opposition by the community, a non-profit was formed and an arrangement was made to save the famed venue.

University of Texas campus
2247 Guadalupe St.
(512) 475-6515
cactuscafe.org

TWO-STEP
AT BROKEN SPOKE

Despite the fact that it now sits smack dab in the middle of a high-rise apartment complex, this little honky-tonk is still a great destination to boot scoot and boogie. This place is as charming as it is inviting, and it's the type of atmosphere that reminds you of the nostalgic "old" Austin.

3201 S. Lamar Blvd.
(512) 442-6189
brokenspokeaustintx.com

SEE WILLIE NELSON
PERFORM LIVE

Willie Nelson wasn't born in Austin, but he got here as soon as he could. He still plays here at least once or twice a year, but he won't live forever! This needs to jump right on up to the top of your priority list.

CATCH A JAZZ SHOW
AT THE ELEPHANT ROOM

The low ceilings and dim lighting at this basement venue on Congress Avenue provide the perfect ambiance for jazz music. This is often my first recommendation for visitors staying downtown. They have awesome jazz acts from Austin and around the globe, seven days a week. Be sure to bring a single dollar bill with you to sign and stick to the ceiling for eternity; the bartenders will gladly allow you to use their stapler.

315 Congress Ave.
(512) 473-2279
elephantroom.com

Perfect night:
Have dinner and drinks upstairs at Swift's Attic, then walk down the steps to the Elephant Room and get lost in great music.

HAVE A GOOD NIGHT
AT THE GOODNIGHT

This is the ultimate adult playground. The food is top notch—think everything from traditional bar food like sliders and pizza to deep-fried alligator. And the extensive cocktail menu has something to please anyone, including infused cocktails and some great craft brews. If you have a designated driver, ask about the "megamugs" and "megamosas"; they're definitely not for lightweights.

After you eat, they have a huge array of activities including vintage bowling lanes, Ping-Pong, shuffleboard, pool, board games, and a karaoke room. They also have plenty of TVs and seating if you want to catch a game. It's a great place for a first date or for a night out with a group of friends.

For a blast from the past, don't forget to stop by the Zoltar machine.

2700 W. Anderson Ln., #101
(512) 459-5000
thegoodnightaustin.com

SPORTS & RECREATION

WATCH THE SUN
CRASH INTO THE HORIZON
AT MOUNT BONNELL

A trip to Mount Bonnell is basically a right of passage for any new Austinite. Upon ascending the hundred or so steps to the top, you'll quickly learn why it's one of the city's best spots to hang out. It's one of Austin's oldest tourist attractions, dating back to the 1850s. It also holds the title of highest point within the city limits, at 785 feet. The view from the top is truly breathtaking; you can see everything, including downtown, the Capitol, the UT Tower, and the 360 Bridge.

3800 Mt. Bonnell Rd.

STRUT YOUR STUFF:
VISIT THE MAYFIELD PARK PEACOCKS

There's something very "Secret Garden" about Mayfield Park. It's a treasure hidden right in the middle of central Austin. The luscious landscape is home to peacocks that stroll the ground like they own it.

3505 W. 35th St., mayfieldpark.org

GO FLY A KITE
AT THE ANNUAL ZILKER KITE FESTIVAL

If you spend any time in Austin, you'll quickly learn that there's a festival for everything. Held yearly on the first Sunday in March, this festival is the city's official feel-good kickoff to spring. There are thousands of kites of all shapes and sizes, including both store-bought and homemade creations. They have contests for most unusual kite, strongest pulling kite, and largest kite, to name a few. While I'm a fan of participating in the event, it's also fun to just lie on the Zilker lawn and watch the thousands of kites swirling overhead. In the weeks following the event, you'll see stray kites strewn about the treetops at Zilker, all waiting for the next big gust of wind.

abckitefestival.com

FIND INNER PEACE
WITH DONATION-BASED YOGA

To many Austinites, yoga is as much a part of the daily routine as a morning cup of joe. There seems to be a yoga studio on every corner, but donation-based yoga is really the way to go. With donation-based yoga, you pay what you can afford while still getting a great workout. Practice Yoga is a new spot that recently opened on the Eastside. The instructors are super friendly and experienced, and the space is simply amazing.

Practice Yoga Austin
1103 E. 6th St.
(512) 730-1638
practiceyogaaustin.com

Black Swan Yoga
1114 W. 5th St., #202
(512) 630-2332
blackswanyoga.com

GET YOUR HORNS UP
AT A TEXAS FOOTBALL GAME

In this land that lacks a professional football team, Longhorn football is king. There's something about being in the stadium that makes you feel alive; perhaps it's the energy of the people filling the over 100,000 stadium seats. There's a camaraderie among Texas fans that can only be understood from inside the stadium. It goes without saying, sport your best burnt orange.

Darrell K Royal Texas–Memorial Stadium
405 E. 23rd St.
(512) 471-7437
texassports.com

GRAB COFFEE
WITH A VIEW AT MOZART'S COFFEE ROASTERS ON LAKE AUSTIN

Mozart's is great for a morning cup of coffee, and even better as a place to get some work done on your laptop. Located on Lake Austin, their deck is truly one of the most tranquil places in the city. In December they take Christmas lights to the extreme with an extravagant display; the entire deck is basically under a canopy of lights. Starting each night at 6:00 P.M., on the hour, there's a pretty incredible light show. This is a fun holiday stop for the entire family, including the canines!

3826 Lake Austin Blvd.
(512) 477-2900
mozartscoffee.com

Tip:

Plan ahead and bring a bottle of wine
for the ultimate sailing experience.

TAKE SAIL
ON LAKE TRAVIS

Did you know that you can take to the calm waters of Lake Travis, no experience needed? Yup, you don't need to be on the coast to test out your sea legs. Just show up ready to learn, and after a brief tutorial (taught by the sweet local couple that owns the place), you'll be ready to set sail. The experience is simply amazing and more relaxing than you can imagine. Luckily, the waters of Lake Travis are pretty calm but breezy so amateurs and experts alike will enjoy navigating the lake.

Austin Sailboat Rentals
austinsailboatrentals.com

RUN, BIKE, OR STROLL
AROUND LADY BIRD LAKE

Lady Bird Lake in many ways is the heart of the city. It separates downtown from South Austin, and is a large part of what makes our city so beautiful. The ten-plus mile trail that borders much of the lake is a highlight for many of the city's active residents. Be sure to wander across the Pfluger Pedestrian Bridge; it's a great place to sit down and take in the city, and it makes for a great downtown photo op as well!

austintexas.gov/page/lady-bird-lake

PLAY
PETER PAN MINI GOLF

Built in 1946, it hasn't changed much since, so you sort of feel like you're stepping back in time when you walk in. There aren't a whole lot of modern-day putt-putt gimmicks, but the course is well maintained and is a ton of fun for all ages. They only accept cash for payment and it's BYOB, so bring a box of wine (no glass) for a pretty awesome date night.

1207 Barton Springs Rd.
(512) 472-1033
peterpanminigolf.com

HIKE
THE BARTON SPRINGS GREENBELT

Thanks to our current drought, nowadays you only see water in the greenbelt in the aftermath of a torrential rainstorm. The trails are less developed than the Town Lake Trail, for example; there are a lot more rocks, roots, and elevation changes. But the people who frequent the greenbelt prefer it that way! It's a great place to hike, and if you consider yourself an outdoorsy type, this should definitely be one of the first activities you check off your list. I suggest parking along the right side of the southbound access road of MoPac (Loop 1), just south of 360 (Capital of Texas Highway). Then just hop on the trail and follow it down the hill!

texasoutside.com/bartongreenbelt.htm

PRACTICE YOUR
SHORT GAME AT
BUTLER PARK PITCH AND PUTT

There aren't many places that make me more appreciative of my city than the course at Butler. It's a small nine-hole golf course tucked into some woods just south of Town Lake, where all of the holes are par threes, so the only clubs you'll need are a wedge and a putter.

You don't even have to like golf to play here—think of it as a step above putt-putt. They even have clubs you can use if you don't have your own. Dogs are welcome, it's BYOB, and at a price of eight bucks a round, Butler can't be beat!

201 Lee Barton Dr.
butlerparkpitchandputt.com

ZIP-LINE
ER LAKE TRAVIS
AT LAKE TRAVIS ZIP LINE ADVENTURES

Imagine zip-lining through the treetops at speeds of up to sixty miles per hour! Lake Travis Zip Line Adventures' course takes you up and down huge hillsides, and even over the lake on one of the lines. The guides are all super friendly, and on the last line there are actually two cables, so you can race against a friend!

Be prepared to get a workout, as you need to hike up a hill before you can zip down one, but the breathtaking views and the exhilaration from the ride make it well worth the effort!

14529 Pocahontas Trl., Volente, Texas 78641
ziplaketravis.com

PITCH A TENT
AT EMMA LONG PARK

There are dozens of great places to camp within twenty minutes of downtown, but Emma Long might take the cake for the best place to camp within city limits. The park sits at water level on Lake Austin. It's also a great place to spend a few hours on any weekend.

Park amenities include picnic tables, volleyball courts, a roped-off swimming area, hiking trails, and more. Park fees are between $5 and $10 a day, and camping spots start at $10.

1706 City Park Rd.
austintexas.gov/department/city-parks

COOL OFF
AT BARTON SPRINGS POOL

If you haven't been here yet, move it to the top of your list. The pool is fed by a natural underground spring that keeps it at a crisp 68 degrees year-round, making it one of the most popular places in the city on hot summer days. It really is a one-of-a-kind place. You'll see people of all ages and all walks of life out here on any given day. Fun fact: Robert Redford learned to swim here.

There's a great hill for sunbathing and some great shade trees as well. They also have a diving board that's popular with kids and grown-ups alike.

Admission is $3 for adults, $2 for ages 12–17, and $1 for kids 11 and under. You can bring towels, reading materials, drinks in re-sealable containers (no alcohol), and not much else. Be sure to check their website for a full list of prohibited items.

2201 Barton Springs Rd.
(512) 476-9044
austintexas.gov/department/barton-springs-pool

TAKE A SELFIE
AT THE 360 OVERLOOK

Easily one of the most popular photo backdrops in the city, the views from the cliffs above the Pennybacker (360) Bridge must be seen in real life to be fully understood. The bridge itself is a beautiful structure, but the downtown skyline and the gorgeous stretch of Lake Austin below really help to bring the panoramic view full circle.

To get there, park on the shoulder right before the bridge when traveling south on Highway 360. It's a short hike up the hill that can easily be trekked in flip-flops.

Loop 360 and Lake Austin
Austin

Tip:

Booking a spa treatment allows access to the rest of the resort during the day without having to spend the extra money to stay at the resort overnight. Weekends get a little hectic so schedule your visit midweek, if possible.

TREAT YOURSELF
AT LAKE AUSTIN SPA

This is the ultimate destination to unwind and rejuvenate. As soon as the gates to the property open, you feel as if you're in paradise. The welcoming staff and serene lakefront atmosphere are instantly calming.

If relaxing by the pool isn't your scene, you're in luck as they have an endless schedule of classes and activities. Options include cooking demos, wine tastings, sailing, kayaking, meditation, hiking, and more. Yoga lovers, be sure to take some time for yourself on the yoga deck above the lake; it's the ultimate in peacefulness.

1705 S. Quinlan Park Rd.
(512) 372-7300
lakeaustin.com/spa-resort

DECOMPRESS
AT DEEP EDDY POOL

Deep Eddy Pool is a must for anyone who wants to call himself or herself an Austinite. It began as a swimming hole in the Colorado River before the Great Depression. Cold springs rose from the riverbanks and people swam in the water where a large boulder formed an eddy. A concrete pool was finally built in 1915. In its heyday, the pool was a carnival-like resort with cabins, camping, concessions, a 50-foot diving platform, a zip line, a slide, and even a Ferris wheel. Ah, to be an Austinite back then—sounds like heaven. I guess the liability of a zip line and a 50-foot diving platform became a little too much for the city.

That's enough history. Let's focus on the present-day Deep Eddy Pool. It's a great spot for all of your swimming needs. The water is constantly around 73 degrees, so be aware that it's on the chilly side. In this Texas heat though, it's very refreshing! They have a section for swimming laps and another for just swimming and playing.

During the summer they have splash movie nights, where they bring in a big movie screen and you can relax in the pool while catching a flick. It's the ultimate way to chill out in Austin's summer heat.

401 Deep Eddy Ave., deepeddy.org

EXPLORE CONCRETE HEAVEN
AT THE VELOWAY

Austin is a city that is always active, and cycling happens to be one of the favorite forms of exercise and transportation for locals. For these reasons, the Veloway is concrete gold.

If biking isn't your thing, the Veloway is now open to rollerblading as well. Yeah, you read that right; go dig out the wheeled shoes of your past and go for a spin. The track consists of 3.1 miles of paved asphalt heaven. Admittedly, for the serious biker a 3.1-mile loop may be a little mundane, but for some Saturday exercise, a little afternoon enjoyment, and excellent scenery, this is your place.

Here are some pointers before you go: the circular loop is twenty-three feet wide, everyone rides in a one-way, clockwise direction, and helmets are required by city ordinance. The Veloway is only for bicycles and rollerblades! Walkers, runners, and hikers are all prohibited.

Seasoned and recreational bikers alike will enjoy this Austin treasure.

4900 La Crosse Ave.
veloway.com

GROW AT THE
SUNSHINE COMMUNITY GARDEN

Sunshine Community Garden was established in 1979 and provides an urban oasis for Austinites to grow their own organic food and flowers.

The land is licensed to them at no cost through the support of the Texas School for the Blind and Visually Impaired. The garden is an all-volunteer organization with no paid staff and it supports education with garden tours, donations of seeds to local youth groups, and by providing a meeting space for other nonprofits.

Every March they host their annual spring plant sale. It's a great way to fill your garden with plants, flowers, and veggies, all while supporting an awesome local organization. Check out their website for more details.

4814 Sunshine Dr.
sunshinecommunitygardens.org

GET WEIRD AT THE
KEEP AUSTIN WEIRD FESTIVAL AND 5K

Our city motto is Keep Austin Weird, so it makes sense that we would have a Keep Austin Weird festival. This festival is the perfect way to experience a lot of Austin in just one day. It brings together everything that we love about Austin: great music, family fun, and local vendors.

If you haven't participated in this one-of-a-kind 5K, it's an anything goes fun run that ends up consisting of a truly eclectic mix of people. Come in costume—the weirder the better.

There are even stops along the way like Amy's Ice Creams, so it's no wonder it's been deemed "the slowest 5K you'll ever run."

keepaustinweirdfest.com

BLOW GLASS

Glassblowing may sound like something best left to the experts. While it probably is, a visit (and perhaps a class) to this gallery is definitely worth the trip. The owners, Shara and Leigh, are true experts and are mesmerizing to watch.

The studio uses recycled glass, so they're constantly collecting old vases, dishes, and other scraps to reuse.

If you want to do more than just spectate, they offer a series of classes, one-time experiences, and private lessons, and they even host bachelorette parties! Needless to say, they just want to get you excited about blowing glass.

My favorite creations are these beautiful bowls made out of recycled glass. They're each one of kind, locally made, and unique. They sell for $25.

You should also take a stroll through their studio, attached to the glassblowing workshop, as it showcases a bunch of their finished products.

3401 E. 4th St.
(512) 815-2569
eastsideglassstudio.com

RED'S SHOOTING RANGE.
JUST GO.

The freedom to shoot a gun is so effortless in Texas; it's a must-do—no excuses.

Never shot a gun before? They offer one-on-one lessons for $50 an hour. Check their site for more details.

6200 U.S. 290
(512) 892-4867
redsguns.com

, CANOE, OR ROW
ON LADY BIRD LAKE

Spend an afternoon on the lake. This dammed portion of the Colorado River restricts the use of boats that have gas engines, so it's nice and calm for paddleboards, hydro-bikes, kayaks, and canoes.

On any given day you'll see dozens of people enjoying this stretch of water, often making me wonder if people in Austin actually work!

My recommendation is to rent your preferred form of transportation late in the afternoon, spend some time exploring the river and then around dusk, head on over to the Congress Bridge to watch the bats fly from below. Bat watching from the lake is a great perspective, and it's fun to watch all the people lined up on the bridge.

austintexas.gov/page/lady-bird-lake

Fact:

You may hear Lady Bird Lake referred to as Town Lake. In 2007 the city changed the name, but to longtime residents it will always be Town Lake.

CULTURE
& HISTORY

VISIT THE BAYL STREET ART WALL

Austin is a city that embraces its street art scene. It's a huge part of the culture and energy that makes this city so special. The mecca for graffiti art in Austin is located on Baylor Street. Years ago, the property was slated to be turned into condos and a concrete foundation was poured. The project never made it past that step, and the barren concrete walls now provide a huge canvas for local artists. After you've spent some time inspecting all of the paintings, climb up to the very top of the wall and check out the amazing view of the city.

11th and Baylor St.

SPIN UNDER THE LIGHTS
OF THE ZILKER HOLIDAY TREE

Spending a December evening twirling around under the Zilker Tree is fun whether you're five or fifty-five. Something about putting your arms out, looking up into the tree and spinning in circles as you watch the lights swirl above you makes you feel like a kid again and maybe a little nauseous if you get too carried away! Spinning under the tree has been a holiday pastime since the 1960s. The tree stands 155 feet tall and includes 3,309 lights formed into a unique spiral pattern by city of Austin electricians. Vendors sell hot chocolate, funnel cakes, and other holiday favorites, and the whole experience is so magical that even if the temperature is in the 80s, you can't help but feel the holiday cheer. The tree lighting takes place the first week of December and runs through New Year's Eve.

austintexas.gov/zilkerholidaytree

DO SOMETHING
THAT REQUIRES A VISIT TO
LUCY IN DISGUISE

If you are doing something that requires a visit to Lucy in Disguise, you know you are in for a real treat. Lucy's is the ultimate costume emporium. They are literally busting at the seams with anything and everything costume related. They offer a seemingly never-ending supply of costumes, wigs, props, makeup, accessories, decorations, jewelry, and boas. Everything you need to transform yourself into whatever or whomever you need to be. As the saying goes, "Everything is bigger in Texas," and Lucy's is no exception. Located on South Congress Avenue, it has become a staple of the street.

1506 South Congress Ave.
(512) 444-2002
lucyindisguise.com

Tip:

Prime bat-watching season is August,
after the moms give birth to their pups.
The young bats join their mothers
on their evening flights.

WATCH THE
CONGRESS AVENUE BRIDGE BATS FLY

The largest urban bat colony in North America calls the Congress Avenue Bridge home. About 1.5 million Mexican free-tail bats live here from spring to early fall as they migrate north from Mexico. Each night around dusk the bats start their evening feeding. It normally starts with a single bat leaving the bridge and quickly turns into a steady flow of countless bats in search of food. It's estimated that each evening the bats consume 10,000 to 30,000 pounds of insects, and it can take up to forty-five minutes for all the bats to leave the confines of the bridge.

For more information and updates on the bats, call the
Bat Conservation International hotline at (512) 327-9721.

While I enjoy watching the bats from either a kayak on the lake or standing on the bridge, you can also go on a bat-watching cruise.

Lonestar Riverboat (512) 327-1388, lonestarriverboat.com
Capital Cruises (512) 480-9264, capitalcruises.com

FIRST THURSDAYS
ON SOUTH CONGRESS

On the first Thursday of every month, South Congress throws the ultimate block party. Most stores south of Barton Springs and north of Elizabeth Street stay open late (until about 10:00 P.M.). Many stores have sales and hand out drinks, and restaurants and bars usually offer other specials on this honorary Thursday. Local vendors set up stands where you can find handcrafted jewelry, art, clothes, and unique Austin artifacts. In the midst of this celebration, you'll find local musicians playing in parking lots, alleys, and on the street corners. The combination of local business, food, drink, and music makes for an enjoyable experience.

DECORATE A TREE
ALONG HIGHWAY 360 IN DECEMBER

While warm days certainly outnumber the cold, nothing deters Austinites from getting into the holiday spirit! Each year there seem to be more and more decorated trees along Highway 360. It's one of those things that makes Austin both unique and eclectic. The story goes that this tradition began around ten years ago with just one tree, decorated under the cover of night by a local family. Every year more and more decorated trees pop up. The tree decorations are just as original as the city's residents. Think everything from traditional ornaments, candy canes, and garland, to funky trees sporting flamingos, rainbows, Barbie dolls, and more. This is just another way we manage to keep Austin weird, one tree at a time.

Important:
After New Year's, make sure to go undecorate your tree. Otherwise, you're just finding a creative way to litter.

SEE THE CITY
FROM ABOVE ON A UNIVERSITY OF TEXAS TOWER TOUR

The University of Texas Tower has one of the best views in town, as you get a 360-degree view of the entire city from over 300 feet up. It's actually taller than the Texas Capitol! Tours are self-guided, but there are student workers at the top to give you the 411 and facts about the structure. Tours are $6 and you must make a reservation by calling (512) 475-6636.

utexas.edu/universityunions/texas-union/scene/tower-tours

Tip:

Try to plan your tour around sunset. The way the light reflects off the campus and downtown buildings is pretty incredible.

STEP INSIDE
A POSTCARD AT HAMILTON POOL

This place looks like the oasis that cartoon characters often see after wandering in the desert for three days. Drive about a half hour west of Austin through the tumbleweed and cactus-rich Texas Hill Country, and then wander down a steep path to what can only be described as a natural grotto, complete with waterfall. It will truly take your breath away the first time you see it.

Be sure to check the Travis County Parks website before heading out, as the pool is often closed for several days after a strong rain. It's a great place to hike and take in year-round, but jumping in the chilly spring-fed pool when it's about 105 degrees out is one of the best feelings in the world.

Bring a camera, towels, and a small cooler if you'd like, but keep in mind that there's a pretty steep walk both up and down from the parking lot. Day passes are $10 per vehicle. Get there early on summer days as the park reaches capacity!

24300 Hamilton Pool Rd., Dripping Springs, Texas 78620
parks.traviscountytx.gov/find-a-park/hamilton-pool

VISIT
THE TEXAS CAPITOL

The overused saying "Everything is bigger in Texas" rings true once again with the state capitol. At 308 feet tall, it's 19 feet taller than the U.S. Capitol in D.C.! Looking up at the dome from the inside is pretty breathtaking. The star in the center at the top of the dome is eight feet in diameter, but looks tiny from so far below. Wandering around on your own is pretty fun, but they also offer both guided and self-guided tours for free. Tours last about forty-five minutes and run year-round. Check out their website for more details.

201 E. 14th St.
(512) 463-5495
tspb.state.tx.us

HANG WITH
THE AUSTIN FACIAL HAIR CLUB

Founded in 2007, this uniquely Austin organization celebrates all things bearded and mustached. The president of the club was featured on the IFC television series *Whisker Wars*.

They sell some really great merchandise (t-shirts, hats, etc.), and their facial hair masterpieces are a real thing of beauty. Follow them on Facebook to find their next public appearance.

austinfacialhairclub.com

WATCH
WITTY WORDPLAY AT
THE ANNUAL O. HENRY PUN-OFF

"Lend us an ear and we'll give you more corn," is how those who attended the first O. Henry Pun-Off World Championships were welcomed in 1977. Now, three decades later, this hilarious, creative, wacky wordplay event has become an Austin staple. Watching this event from the audience is pure entertainment on its own, but if you think you have what it takes, registration to compete is open to the public.

Proceeds from the annual event benefit the O. Henry and Dickinson Museums. As far as fund-raisers go, this one is pretty unique.

punpunpun.com

RELISH IN RETRO
AT ROADHOUSE RELICS

Roadhouse Relics is a gallery dedicated to vintage neon designs, and Todd Sanders' handmade crafts have earned him quite the celebrity clientele, including Willie Nelson, Kings of Leon, and ZZ Top. He's also responsible for the signage at famous local spots such as Threadgill's and Doc's.

Purchasing one of his treasures may be out of the question, but visiting the gallery is still worth the trip just to see the detail that goes into them.

Don't miss the famous "Greetings from Austin" mural on the side of the building.

1720 S. 1st St.
(512) 442-6366
roadhouserelics.com

CHICKEN SH*T BINGO
(YES, YOU READ THAT CORRECTLY)

Only in Austin do we play a form of bingo in which the winner is chosen by where a caged chicken decides to relieve itself. This is authentic Austin, dive-bar gloriousness at its finest.

While the bingo gets going around 5 P.M., most people get there early to tailgate, and by 4 P.M. the joint is pretty packed. As if an event titled Chicken Shit Bingo wasn't enough to get you out here, on Sundays they serve free hot dogs with all the fixins.

Keep Austin Weird, y'all.

Ginny's Little Longhorn
5434 Burnet Rd.
(512) 524-1291
thelittlelonghornsaloon.com

PICTURES
IN BLUEBONNETS

Each spring the state flower of Texas blossoms for a few weeks, and fields of these flowers become the backdrop for family photos everywhere. You suddenly notice cars pulled over along the highway with passengers posing on hillsides or even in center medians. While non-Texans may not see the allure of this fabulous flower, true Texans can't help but feel a little bit of excitement.

When the bluebonnets are in peak season, there are countless places to take pictures. My favorite location is on the St. Edward's University campus. There's a hill on the corner of St. Edwards & University Loop Drive that is always covered in bluebonnets, and if you climb up the hill you can get a great view of downtown too!

TAKE A PEDICAB

Traveling by pedicab in Austin is something you have to do at least once. They're the horse-drawn carriages of our city.

On weekends, pedicabs are everywhere downtown, and they offer an environmentally friendly way to get from point A to point B. Some drivers have their cabs decorated with lights or add music to the experience, and I've even seen one decked out in *Star Wars* paraphernalia! Negotiate a flat rate before your ride.

VISIT
THE LYNDON BAINES JOHNSON LIBRARY AND MUSEUM

The Lyndon Baines Johnson Library and Museum on the University of Texas campus is a must-do on your Austin museum tour. The library has the highest visitation of any presidential library.

The top floor of the library has a seven-eighths-scale replica of the Oval Office as it was decorated during Johnson's presidency—one of the coolest parts if you ask me. The library houses 45 million pages of historical documents, 650,000 photos, and 5,000 hours of recordings from the president's political career. A stop by the museum is a great way to spend an afternoon and to gather a bit of American history and culture.

University of Texas campus
2313 Red River St., lbjlibrary.org

Random Fact:
President Johnson graduated from Texas State University (formerly known as Southwest Texas State). He's the only president to graduate from a college in Texas.

SEE TRASH
BECOME TREASURE AT THE CATHEDRAL OF JUNK

The Cathedral of Junk was started in 1988 with a few hubcaps on a fence post. Twenty-five years later, it's turned into a graveyard for lawn mower wheels, car bumpers, cables, bicycle parts, beer signs, and more. It's basically an entire collection of junk-turned-art that you have to see to believe.

It's free to stop by and check out, but donations are accepted. This is the ultimate form of recycling—trash turned to treasure.

4422 Lareina Dr.
(512) 299-7413

CELEBRATE
THE BIRTHDAY OF ALL BIRTHDAYS: EEYORE'S BIRTHDAY

Eeyore's birthday is an annual party that could only happen in Austin, Texas.

This birthday takes place in late April each year and is a celebration of the famously grumpy Winnie the Pooh character. And while we all love Eeyore, this celebration is also for a good cause, benefiting local nonprofit groups.

The vibe of the festival is very 1970s. It's a day of dancing, drum circles, wearing ridiculous costumes (or practically nothing at all), and just enjoying the outdoors. There's a costume contest, temporary tattoo artists, food and drinks, and dozens of other awesome activities.

The festivities are fun for the entire family. It's one of Austin's most popular annual events, and if you're looking for a taste of the city's culture, this is a great way to dive right in!

Pease Park
1100 Kingsbury St.
eeyores.org

BECOME ONE
WITH NATURE AT
ZILKER BOTANICAL GARDEN

Zilker Botanical Garden is a go-to place for relaxing and re-charging. It's one of the most peaceful places in the city, and it's only five minutes from downtown. This is one of the things I love most about Austin: you can be downtown, cross a bridge, and find yourself on a hike and bike trail or in a canoe along Lady Bird Lake.

In 1955 the Austin Area Garden Center was established to support the Zilker Botanical Garden's mission to promote the education and love of gardening among all ages. Nowadays, half a million people from all over the world visit the garden each year.

The grounds are much bigger than one might expect, and the tranquil setting is just incredible. A few of my favorite areas are the Japanese Garden, the Butterfly Trail, and the Herb and Fragrance Garden.

2200 Barton Springs Rd.
(512) 477-8672
zilkergarden.org

VISIT
...AUF SCULPTURE GARDEN AND MUSEUM

The Umlauf Sculpture Garden is located across from Zilker Park and features sculptures by twentieth-century American sculptor Charles Umlauf and other contemporary sculptors. The bronze sculptures in the garden have been waxed so visitors who are blind can use their sense of touch to experience them.

If this serene oasis wasn't enough on a normal day, they also occasionally offer yoga!

605 Robert E. Lee Rd.
(512) 445-5582
umlaufsculpture.org

EMBRACE YOUR
FREE SPIRIT AT HIPPIE HOLLOW

Hippie Hollow is a park that sits on the banks of Lake Travis. What makes it different than any other park, you ask? It's the only clothing-optional public park in the great state of Texas. This remote section on the lake has been a favorite spot for skinny dippers since the 1960s. Park usage is restricted to those eighteen and up.

7000 Comanche Trl.
hippiehollow.com

LEAVE AUSTIN
(NOT FOREVER!)

With so many cool attractions within an hour or so of downtown, it would be a shame not to check out these other Central Texas towns for a day or a weekend.

GRUENE, TEXAS – While technically in the city of New Braunfels, the Gruene Historic District is a place you can easily spend an entire day. The downtown square is peppered with shops, restaurants, and even a quaint little wine bar. Opt for dinner at the cotton gin turned restaurant, the Gristmill, then dance the night away at historic Gruene Hall.

LOCKHART, TEXAS – Austin may be the Live Music Capital of the World, but Lockhart is historically the Barbecue Capital of Texas. The big three are Blacks BBQ, Kreuz BBQ, and Smitty's Market. Tip: Kreuz BBQ's claim to fame is that their BBQ is so good it doesn't need any sauce. You can be the judge of that!

FREDERICKSBURG, TEXAS – This enchanting German town is one of my favorite places to get away. Spring is the best time to go, as the highway on the way to Fredericksburg is lined with beautiful wild flowers for most of the trip. While there, check out Alamo Springs Cafe burgers. You'll have to ask a local how to find it as it's not Google map–able, but trust me, it's worth seeking out.

The town is famous for its vineyards, and a majority of them have free (or cheap) tasting options. A few of my favorites are Bell Mountain Vineyards, the Fredericksburg Winery, and Torre di Pietra Winery.

BULLOCK TEXAS
STATE HISTORY MUSEUM

Texans are proud, so it seems only natural that we would erect a massive museum to honor our state. The Bullock Texas History Museum is a three-story tribute to all things Texas. You can wander through the various levels and get lost in Texas history, artifacts, and culture, while learning "the story of Texas." Each exhibit provides a better understanding of what makes this state so great.

Outside the museum, there's a massive thirty-five-foot bronze star sculpture that creates a great photo opportunity!

The museum also houses Austin's only IMAX theater.

1800 Congress Ave.
(512) 936-8746
thestoryoftexas.com

SCARE YOURSELF
ON AN AUSTIN GHOST TOUR

Austin Ghost Tours have two scary adventures for you to choose from: Ghosts of the Capitol, and Old Pecan Street Ghosts of the Warehouse District.

These ninety-minute walking tours are very informational, providing well-researched Austin and Texas history while also telling the true and sometimes frightening stories of the people, places, and events of Austin's past. Each tour highlights different stories, and the tour guides are amazing storytellers. Both tours promise to give you goose bumps!

(512) 853-9826
austinghosttours.com

BROWSE ART
AT THE BLANTON MUSEUM OF ART

The Blanton Museum of Art of the University of Texas houses the largest and most comprehensive collection of art in Central Texas. The collections range from modern art to centuries-old historical pieces. My favorite thing to do is to bring a pad and pencil and attempt to recreate some of the drawings on my own. I'm a horrible artist, but it's still a lot of fun and a great way to fully appreciate the works of art in front of you! Admission on Thursdays is always free.

200 E. Martin Luther King Jr. Blvd.
(512) 471-7324
blantonmuseum.org

Tip:

You could do this museum and
the Bullock Texas State History Museum
on the same day, as they're located
across the street from each other.

SHOPPING
& FASHION

STOP IN
WATERLOO RECORDS

Austin is famous for being the Live Music Capital of the World, but it's also home to a great institution of recorded music. Waterloo Records gets it's name from the original colony of Waterloo that sat approximately where the northern end of the Congress Avenue Bridge sits today. The practice that originally made them popular was that you could listen to any album in the store before you purchased it, and they had a ten-day, no-questions-asked return policy. They still honor these policies today. Waterloo Records has the best selection of vinyl in the city, as well as rare DVDs and other music memorabilia. Buzzfeed.com recently named them one of the best record stores in the world! Be sure to check their website for their free in-store performances. They have a lot of big-name artists come through, and there are often free refreshments.

600A N. Lamar Blvd.
(512) 474-2500
waterloorecords.com

ЈOT SCOOT
ЯШ Ѕ OVER TO ALLEN'S BOOTS

Those outside of Texas sometimes think we ride horses to work on a trail peppered with cacti. While true in some parts of the state, that's not the case for most people in Austin. We do still love a great pair of cowboy boots though!

Allen's boot superstore has been the go-to place for boots in Austin since 1977, with a selection of over four thousand boots! Movie and rock stars alike have been known to browse the seemingly endless selection. Just look for the huge red boot above their door when you're walking down South Congress Avenue.

1522 South Congress Ave.
(512) 447-1413
allensboots.com

SEARCH
FOR THRIFTY TREASURES
AT UNCOMMON OBJECTS

Uncommon Objects is an endless emporium of antiques, trinkets, and treasures. You'll feel as though you're in your grandma's house sifting through knickknacks that all come with their own unique meanings and stories. The store is actually a collection of multiple vendors who bring their own distinctive touch to the uncommon vibe. Beware: if antiquing is one of your hobbies, you're sure to spend hours roaming these shelves.

1512 South Congress Ave.
(512) 442-4000
uncommonobjects.com

BE A BOOKWORM
AT BOOKPEOPLE

BookPeople is a massive bookstore in the heart of downtown Austin. This multiple-floor collection of books is one of my favorite places in the city. With a knowledgeable staff, café, and endless events, no visit to Austin is complete without browsing their shelves.

Pay attention to the note cards taped under many of the books; these staff critiques are often almost as good as (maybe sometimes better than) the books themselves.

They are constantly hosting events and book readings. Many authors, including Jimmy Carter, Bill Clinton, Lauren Conrad, and Rachel Ray, have had events or signings at the store.

603 N. Lamar Blvd.
(512) 472-5050
bookpeople.com

SUGGESTED ITINERARIES

MUSIC LOVERS

DATE NIGHT

FOODIE FUN

• •

FUN WITH KIDS

KEEP AUSTIN WEIRD

• •

LETS GET ACTIVE

BOTTOMS UP

UNIVERSITY OF TEXAS

ACTIVITIES
BY SEASON

WINTER

SPRING

● ●

SUMMER

FALL

Index

Lastly, a special thank you to Jason Neff who helped me write, edit, and keep my sanity throughout this entire process.